# Our American Family™

# I Am
# Polish
# American

Samuel Kapowski

The Rosen Publishing Group's
**PowerKids Press**™
New York

*To Len—the best friend an author ever had.*

Published in 1997 by The Rosen Publishing Group, Inc.
29 East 21st Street, New York, NY 10010

First Edition

Book Design: Erin McKenna

Photo Credits: Cover © Dusty Willison/International Stock Photo; p. 4 © Mark Bolster/International Stock Photo; pp. 7, 20 © Travelpix/FPG International Corp.; p. 8 © Bettmann Archive; p. 11 © FPG International Corp.; p. 12 © Balfour Walker/FPG International Corp.; pp. 15, 16 © Michael Philip Manheim/International Stock Photo; p. 19 © Chuck Mason/International Stock Photo.

Kapowski, Samuel.
    I am Polish American / by Samuel Kapowski.
       p.    cm. — (Our American Family)
    Includes index.
    Summary: A Polish-American child talks about aspects of his Polish heritage, including foods, customs, and famous Poles.
    ISBN 0-8239-5010-7
    1. Polish Americans—Juvenile literature. [1. Polish Americans.] I. Title. II. Series.
E184.P7T87 1997
973'.049185—dc21                             96-54230
                                                  CIP
                                                     AC

Manufactured in the United States of America

# Contents

# My Grandparents

Hi. My name is Stan. My family is Polish American. My grandmother came to the United States from Poland when she was 25. She moved to a small town in Wisconsin. That's where she met my grandfather, who had also come to the U.S. from Poland.

My grandparents talk about growing up in Poland. They often speak Polish with each other. They teach my cousins and me about Polish history and **culture** (KUL-cher). My parents and grandparents have taught me to be proud of being Polish American.

◀ You can learn a lot about your heritage by spending time with your parents or grandparents.

# Poland

Poland is in the middle of Europe. It has flat, **fertile** (FER-tul) land. Many Polish people work on farms. They grow potatoes, beets, and wheat. The word *pole* means field in Polish. People from Poland are also called Poles.

Warsaw is the capital of Poland. It is a large, **historic** (his-TOR-ik) city. Warsaw is split into two parts. One part, called Old Town, has narrow streets and beautiful, old houses. The New Town is very modern. Some of my Polish cousins work in tall office buildings in New Town.

Some of the buildings in the Old Town section of Warsaw were built during the 1300s! ▶

# A Great Hero

Tadeusz Kosciuszko is a great Polish hero. He believed in **liberty** (LIB-er-tee) and human rights for all people. In 1777 he went to America to help the **colonists** (KOL-uh-nists) fight for freedom in the Revolutionary War. He also started a school for African Americans.

In 1794, Tadeusz returned to Poland. There, he led the Polish people in a battle against countries that had taken their land. The Polish people lost the fight, but Tadeusz never stopped believing that freedom was meant for all people.

◄ Tadeusz Kosciuszko is a famous war hero in Poland and the United States.

# Fighting for Land

In the 1790s, Poland's neighbors, Russia, Prussia, and Austria, took most of Poland's land. The Polish people had to live under the rule of these countries. Over the years, Poland has had to struggle for its **independence** (in-dee-PEN-dents).

In the 1940s, during World War II, things were very bad in Poland. Germany and Russia both tried to take over Polish land. There was a lot of fighting and millions of Poles were killed. This is when my grandmother came to the United States. Today, Poland has its own land and rules itself.

Many countries have tried to take over Poland's land and cities through war. ▶

# The Pope

One of the most famous living Polish people today is Pope John Paul II. His given name is Karol Wojtyla. He was born in Wadowice, a city in southern Poland. That is where my grandmother was born.

Karol became a priest in 1945. He was elected Pope John Paul II, the leader of the Roman Catholic Church, in 1978. He is the first Polish pope. He has traveled all around the world to speak to and pray with millions of people. My family and I saw the pope when he came to the United States.

◀ Millions of people gather to see Pope John Paul II lead a religious service.

13

# Pulaski Day Parade

Pulaski Day is a Polish holiday that my family celebrates. It was started in 1937 to honor Count Casimir Pulaski, who fought in the American Revolutionary War. There is a parade in New York City to honor this day.

Many Polish Americans wear **traditional** (truh-DISH-un-ul) Polish clothing and march in the parade with bands and colorful floats. My mother went to the Pulaski Day Parade when she was younger. She cheered as the bands passed by and she listened to the lively **polkas** (POL-kuhs) that were played.

After the Pulaski Day Parade, some Polish Americans celebrate with family and friends. These people are ▶ dancing a polka.

14

# Dressing Up for Holidays

Some Polish Americans wear traditional clothes for celebrations and holidays. Women wear colorful skirts and white blouses. They also wear brightly **embroidered** (em-BROY-derd) aprons over their skirts. Polish embroidery usually shows scenes from nature, with many birds and flowers. Polish women often wear flowers and ribbons in their hair.

Polish men wear brightly striped trousers tucked into their boots. Red and black boots are also popular. My father gave me his black boots, but they are still too big for me.

◀ Many Polish Women add a colorful, beaded necklace to their traditional outfit.

17

# Food

Kielbasa (kil-BAS-ah), or smoked sausage, is one of Poland's most popular dishes. Pierogis (peer-OH-geez) are also very popular. Pierogis are dumplings that can be stuffed with meat, cabbage, potatoes, or cheese.

For holidays my grandmother makes *babka* (BAHB-kah). *Babka* is a delicious bread made with raisins or prunes. My favorite dessert is ***pacziki*** (pak-ZEE-kee). These are doughnuts filled with jelly and rolled in sugar. My father taught me how to make *pacziki*.

The dough for pierogis has to be rolled out with a rolling pin. ▶

# A Polish Wedding

A Polish wedding is a time for great celebration. Many years ago, Polish weddings lasted several days. Today, they sometimes last a weekend. Family and friends travel long distances to wish the bride and groom well.

In Polish villages, brides and grooms wear traditional wedding clothes. At my cousin's wedding, she and her new husband took part in an old tradition. They walked around the dining table three times for good luck. I hope it worked!

◀ Sometimes the guests at a Polish wedding dress in traditional clothing too.

# Great Poles

Marie Curie, the scientist who discovered **radioactivity** (RAY-dee-oh-ak-TIV-ih-tee), was Polish. So was the famous composer Frederic Chopin.

Over 15 million Polish Americans live in the United States. I admire a Polish American named Senator Barbara Mikulski. She was the first woman ever to win a **statewide** (STAYT-wyd) election in Maryland. I hope to work someday in the government just like her.

Polish people have made a difference in the United States and the world.

22

# Glossary

*babka* (BAHB-kah)  A Polish bread made with raisins or prunes.

**colonist** (KOL-uh-nist)  A person who moves to a new country but stays under the rule of his or her own country.

**culture** (KUL-cher)  The beliefs, customs, and religions of a group of people.

**embroider** (em-BROY-der)  To sew designs onto cloth for decoration.

**fertile** (FER-tul)  Good for crops to grow in.

**historic** (his-TOR-ik)  To be famous or important in history.

**independence** (in-dee-PEN-dents)  The freedom to rule oneself.

**kielbasa** (kil-BAS-ah)  Polish smoked sausage.

**liberty** (LIB-er-tee)  The freedom, right, and power to do as one wants.

*pacziki* (pak-ZEE-kee)  Polish doughnuts filled with jelly.

**pierogi** (peer-OH-gee)  A Polish dumpling stuffed with meat, cabbage, potatoes, or cheese.

**polka** (POL-kuh)  The music for a lively eastern European dance.

**radioactivity** (RAY-dee-oh-ak-TIV-ih-tee)  The energy that is given off from tiny parts of certain metals.

**statewide** (STAYT-wyd)  Involving the whole state.

**traditional** (truh-DISH-un-ul)  Customs or beliefs handed down from parent to child.

# Index